What We Have in Common

A Brim Coloring Book

Written by Jane Landey
Edited by David Austin

Drawings by David Austin and Jane Austin

Copyright©2017

Published by CreateSpace: An Amazon Company.

Printed in U.S.A.

Introduction

What We Have in Common Brim Coloring Books enable children color the drawings as they read along! The books display the similarities of related animals. In this series, the bat and the rat are compared. The facts enable children to appreciate common values. Thus, imbibing in them interest towards animals which could make them to appreciate what they have in common with one another.

The Bat

And

The Rat

The bat and the rat have things in common. They are animals with small bodies. They have small ears and the same shape of mouth.

The bat and the rat meet in
a house.

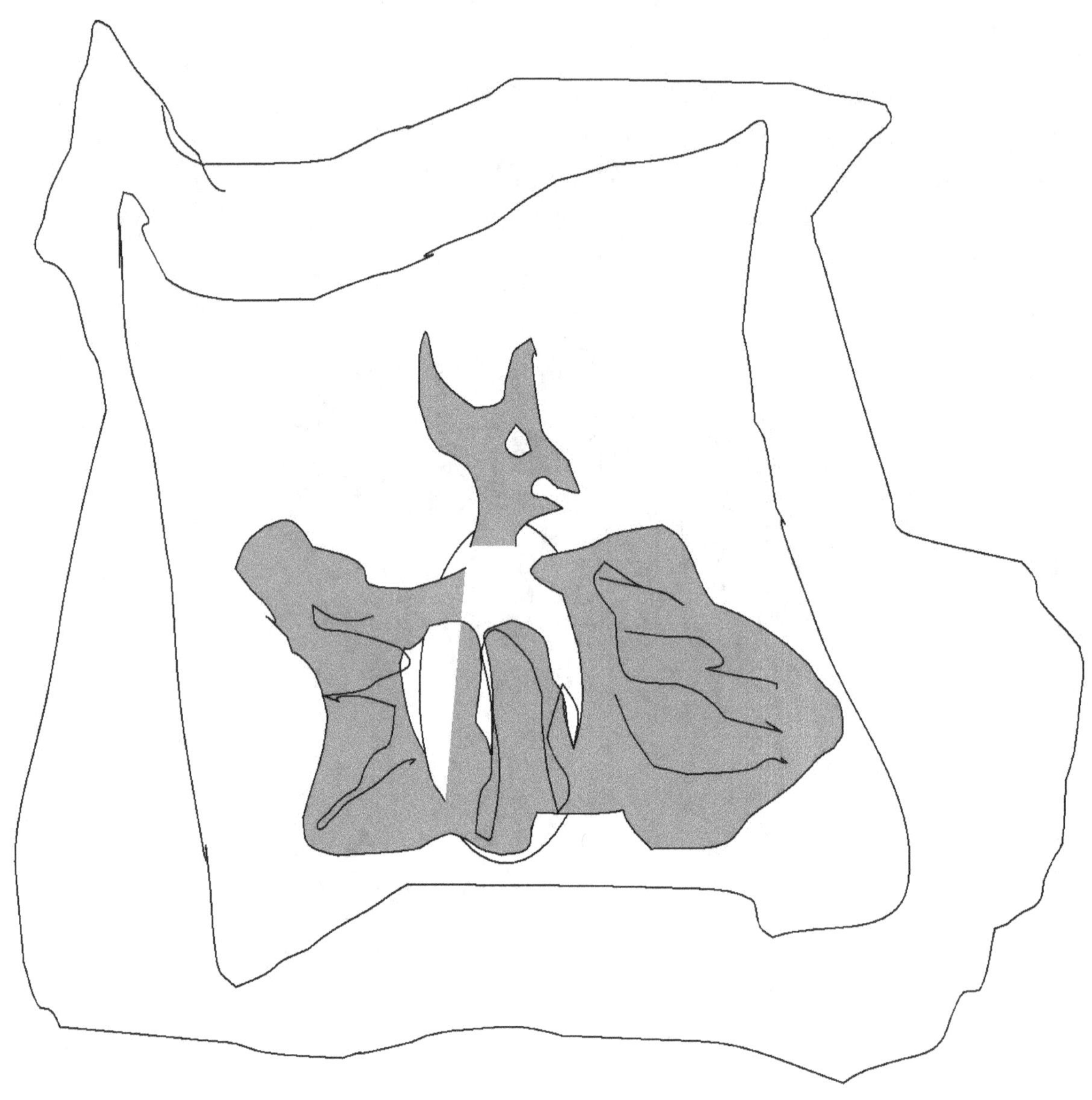

I am a bat.

I am a rat.

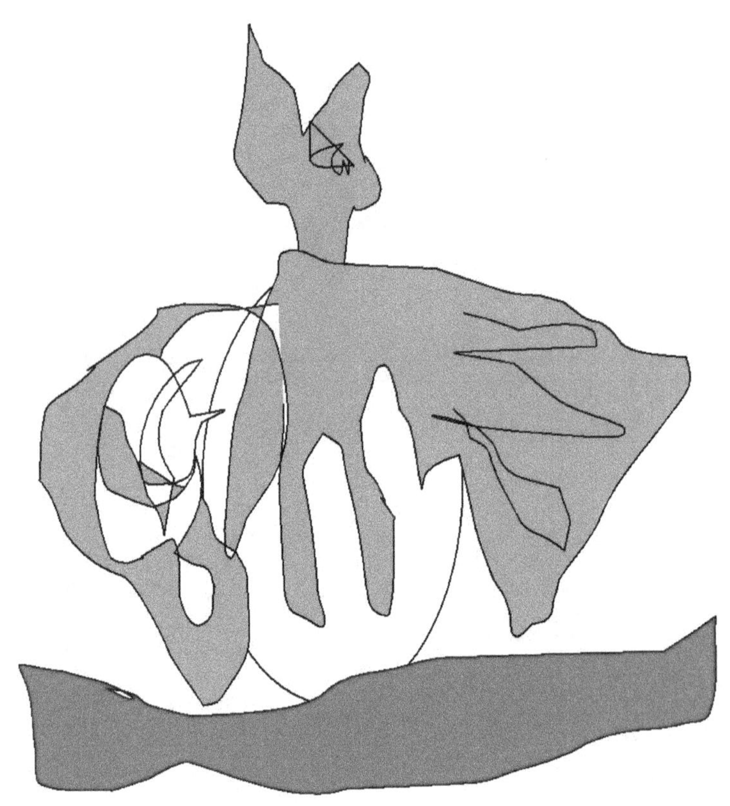

I have small nice ears.

I have small nice ears too!

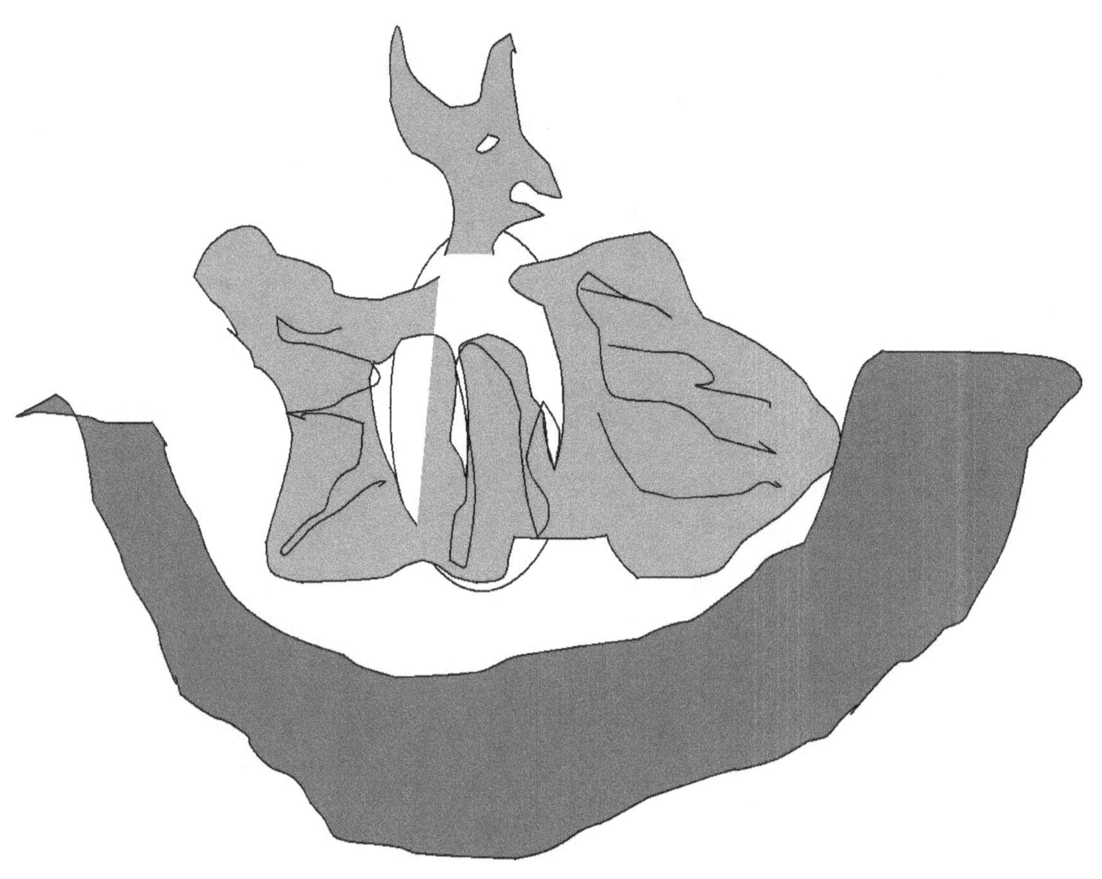

My mouth is small.

My mouth is small too!

I smell with my nose.

I smell with my nose too!

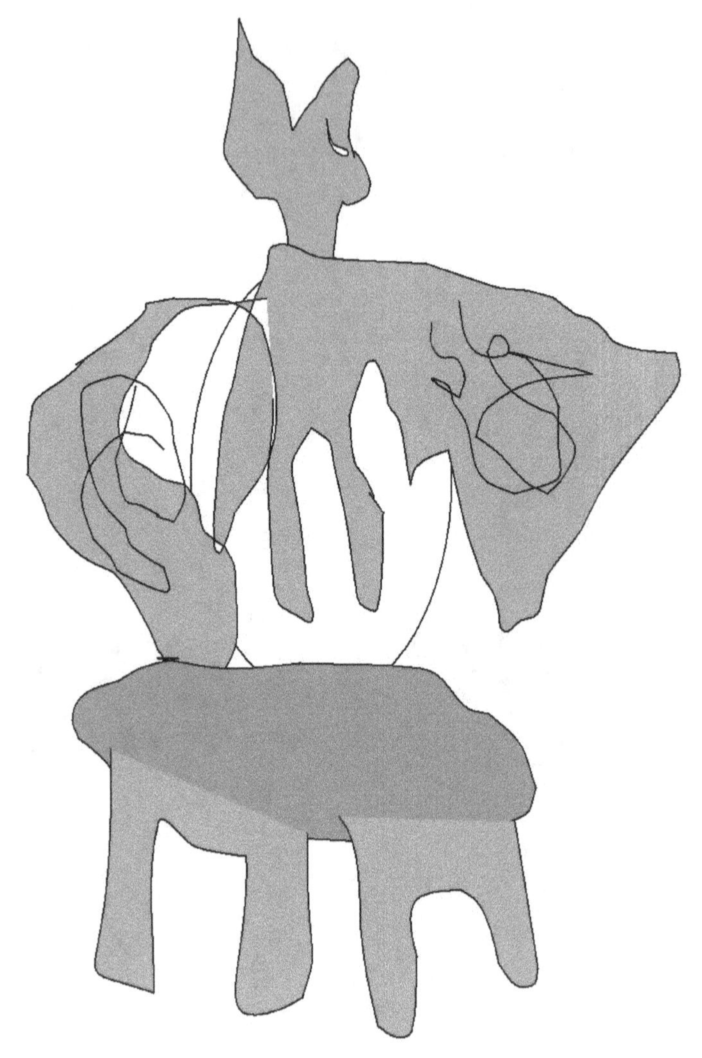

I hold food with my tiny nails.

So do I!

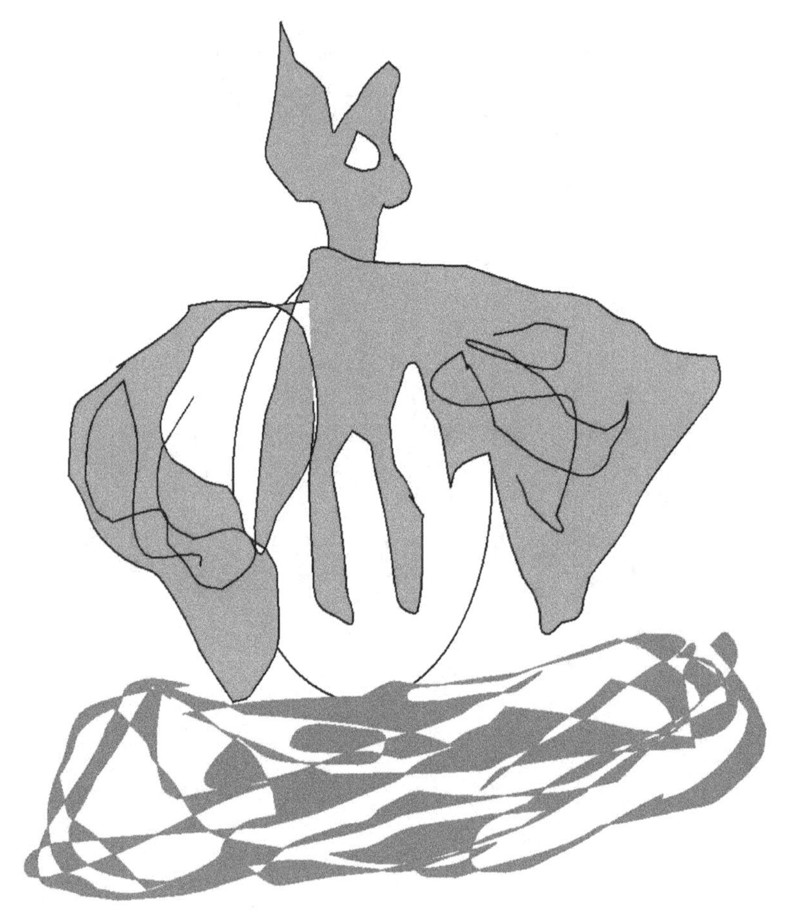

I eat fruits.

I eat grains!

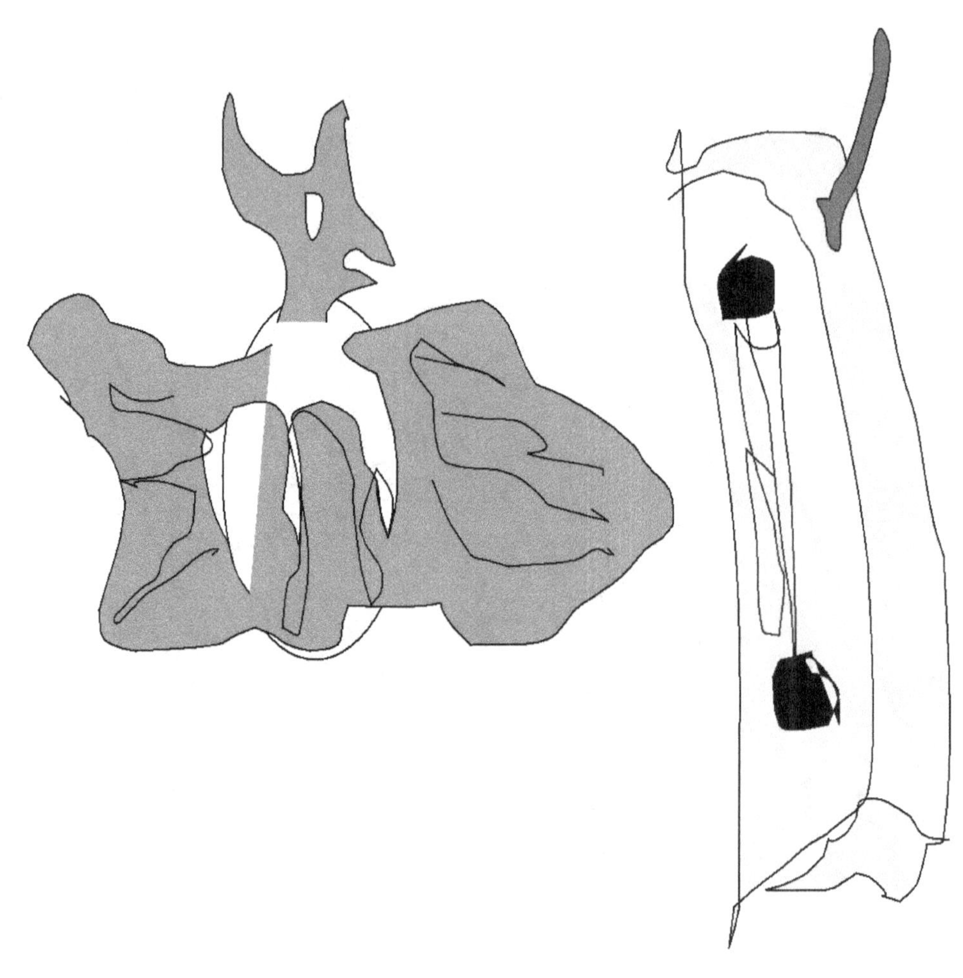

I listen to sound.

I listen to sound too!

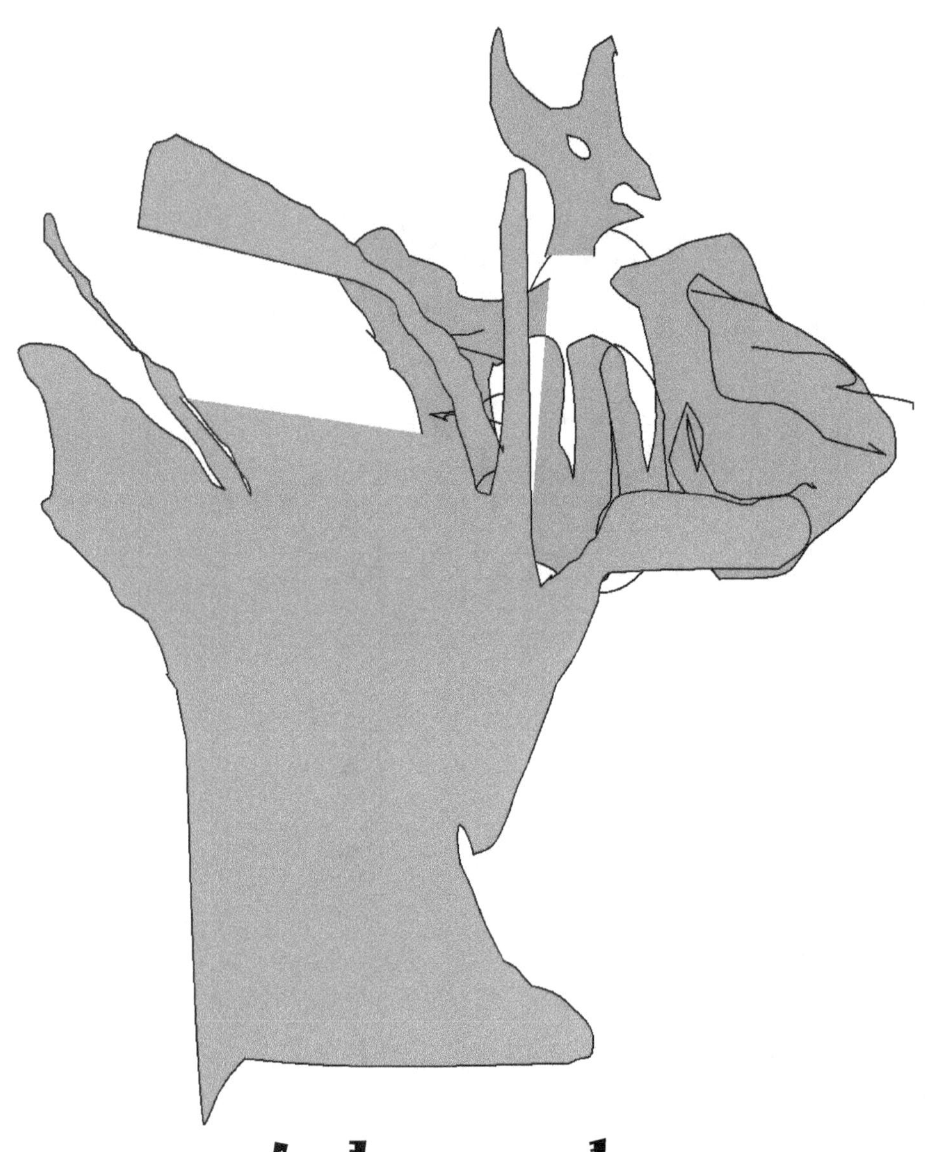

I play on the tree.

I play on shelves too!

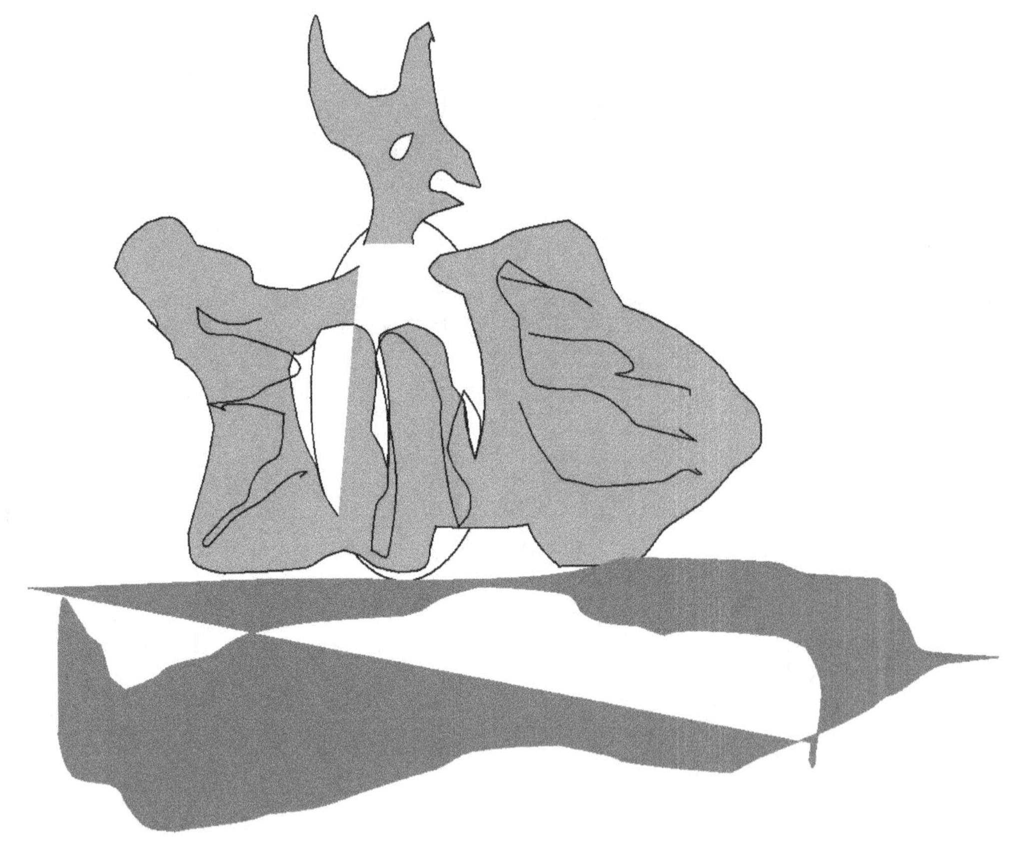

Can you dance?

Yes I can!

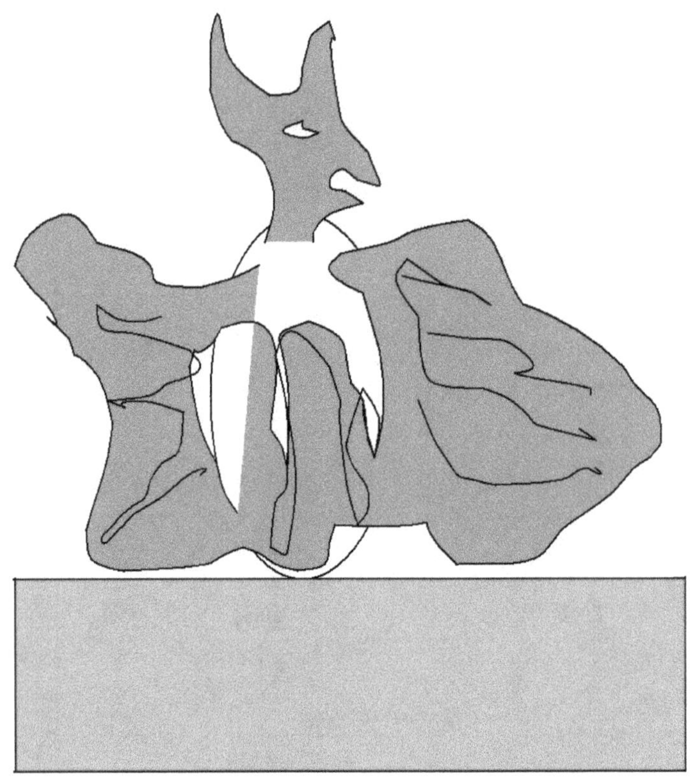

Let's dance!

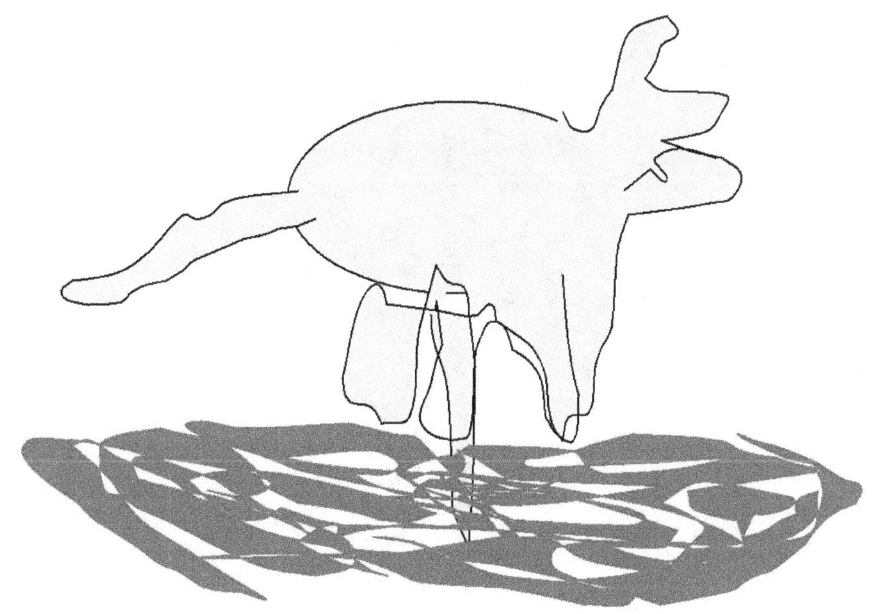

Alright!

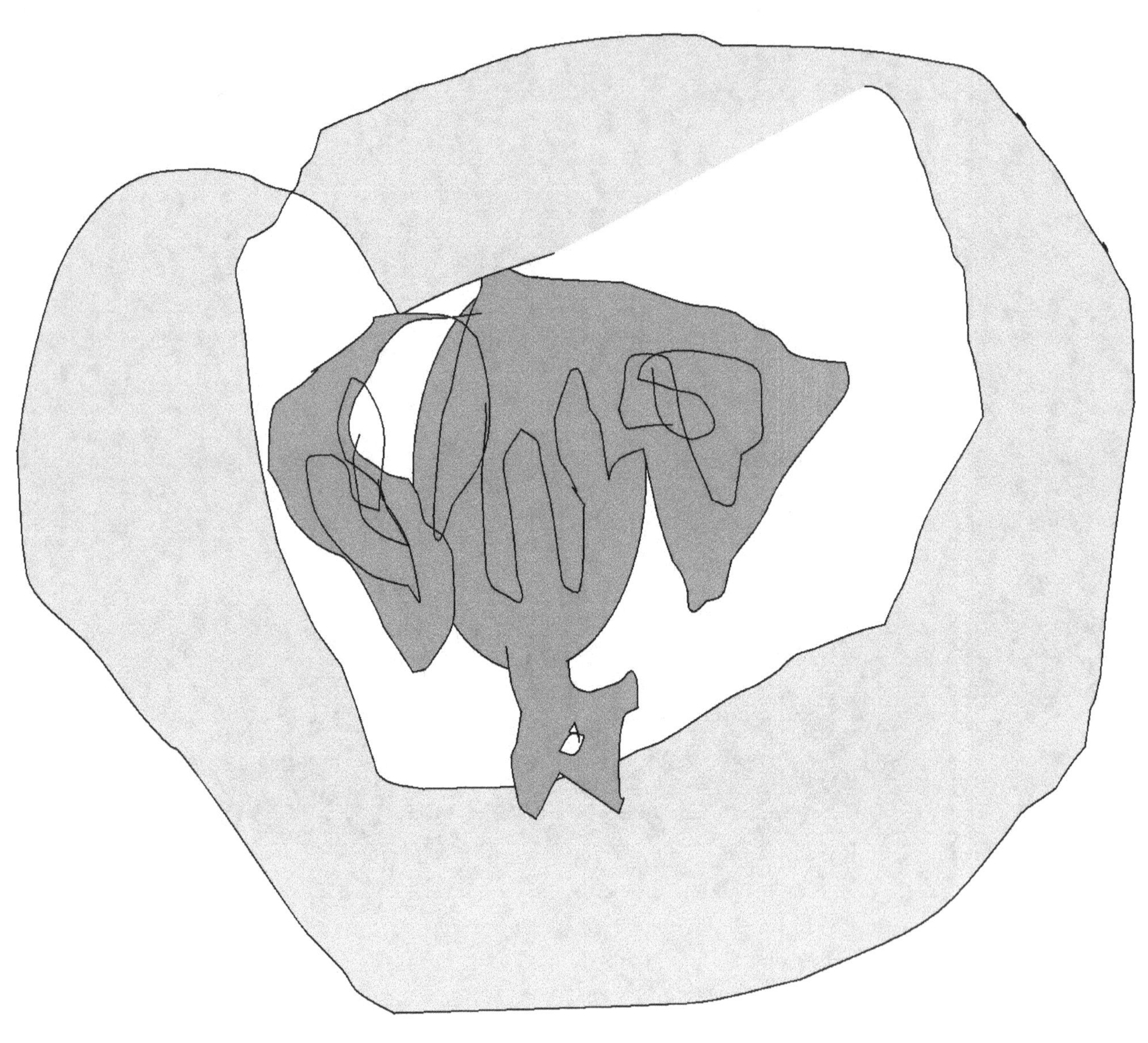

We must dance here every day!

Yes we must.

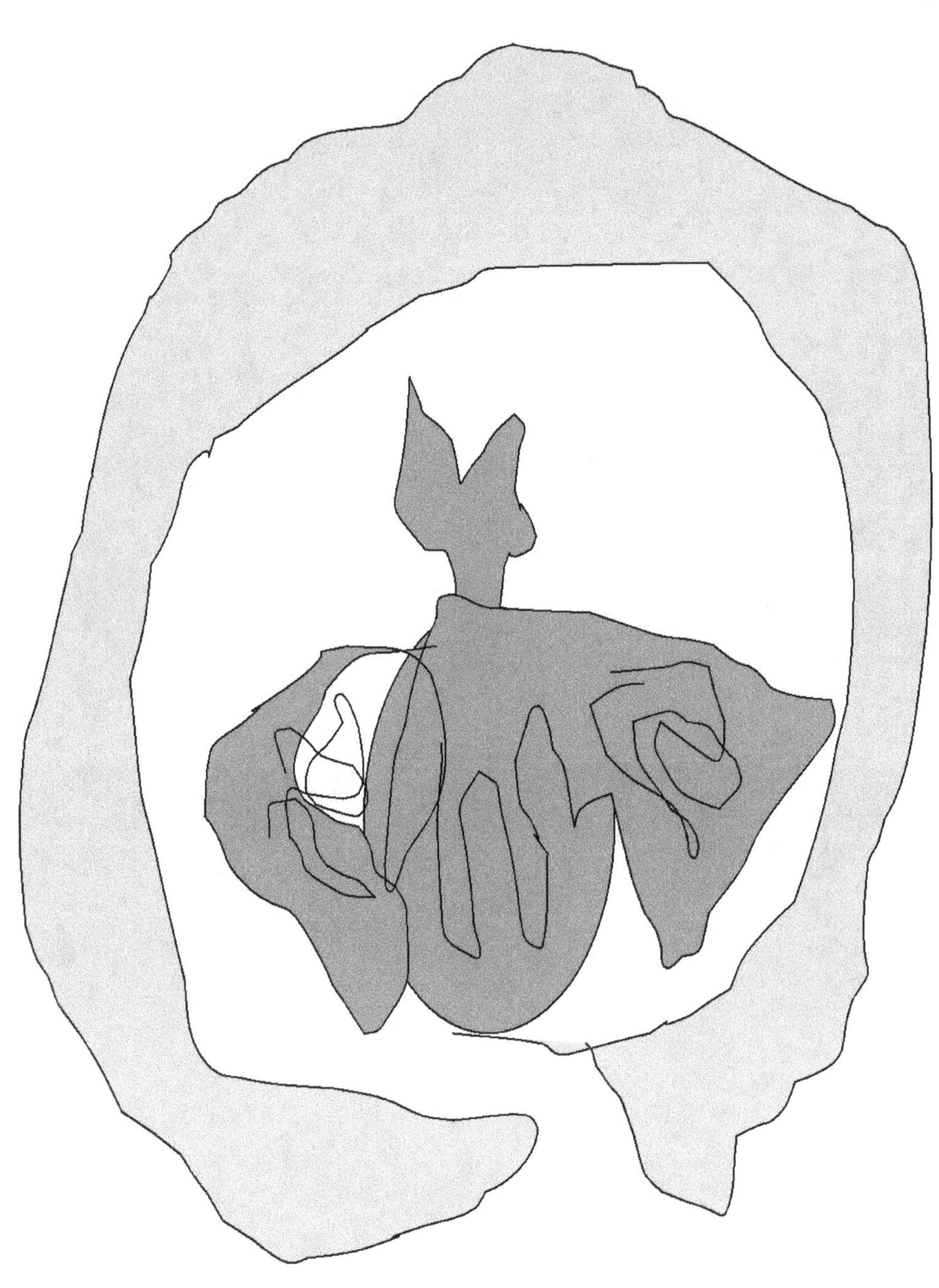

Bye!

Bye!

See you soon Rat

What We Have in Common Brim Coloring Books

Crocodile and Alligator
Turtle and Tortoise
Starfish and Octopus
Worm and Snake
Turkey and Vulture
Ostrich and Emu
Weka and Kiwi
Bat and Rat
Camel and Llama
Duck and Pelican
Kangaroo and Wallaby
Pig and Tapir
Skunk and Squirrel
Hedge and Anteater
Cat and Owl
Elephant and Rhinoceros
Dog and Fox
Buffalo and Bull
Leopard and Cheetah
Horse and Zebra

www.ingramcontent.com/pod-product-compliance
Lightning Source LLC
Chambersburg PA
CBHW081743280726
48660CB00021B/3516